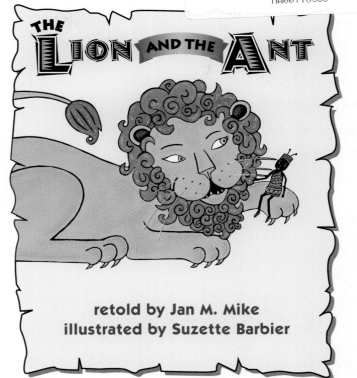

THE LION AND THE ANT

retold by Jan M. Mike
illustrated by Suzette Barbier

MODERN CURRICULUM PRESS

Pearson Learning Group

The jungle rang with exciting news. Lion had been chosen king of the beasts. All the animals, insects, and birds were invited to a grand celebration.

The Ant Queen, though, was too ill to go. So she called her youngest daughter to her side.

"Child, you must take my place at Lion's celebration," she said. "Be patient and respectful so you do not anger Lion."

"Be wise and determined as well so Lion cannot ignore you," she continued. "Show Lion that ants can be powerful friends."

Ant set off. The journey to see Lion was
long and difficult, but Ant was determined to
complete it.

By the time she finally arrived at the celebration, Ant was tired and thirsty. She washed in a cold stream nearby and drank her fill, then she looked around her.

Never had she seen so many different animals, birds, and insects. The air hummed with anticipation. Ant felt very small in the large, noisy crowd.

A long line of animals had formed. Each animal was waiting to bow to the king. Ant joined the end of the line. None of the other animals would even look at her, though.

As Ant waited patiently, Leopard stepped in front of her and swished his powerful tail.

Ant flew up into the air.

Ant tumbled into a mud puddle and climbed out covered with mud. Macaw spread his beautiful blue feathers and laughed.

Then Cobra slithered up.

"Go home, little Ant. You're too small to be important," he hissed. "No one wants to see you bow before Lion."

Ant wiped the mud from her shiny legs as she clicked in bitter frustration.

What should she do? She was too small to fight back against Leopard. Challenging him would be foolish.

Was Cobra right? Was she simply too small to be important? Should she go home and tell her mother she had failed?

Ant decided she would stay because her mother trusted her to do this important job. Ant was determined to bow to Lion. She knew she would find a way to show Lion that ants could be powerful friends.

Soon she was joined by a little green worm.

"May I wait with you?" Worm asked. "My father sent me, but no one will talk to me," the little worm said bitterly.

"Yes," Ant said, "and I'll talk to you."

The line moved slowly as the sun continued to beat down on them. Each animal reached the head of the line, bowed to Lion, and withdrew. Finally, only Ant and Worm were left.

Ant walked up to Lion's throne, but before she could bow, Lion gave a ferocious roar.

"I am tired of all this bowing! Go away, little Ant! You are too small to matter."

Lashing his tail, Lion leaped off his throne.

It was a bitter ending to the day, which made Ant angry. Even the new king thought she was too small to be important.

"What shall I do?" Worm asked. "Should I go home and tell my father I failed?"

"Let's get a good night's sleep first," Ant answered. "Tomorrow may bring us another chance to greet the king."

Worm crept away to find a warm place to nap. Ant curled up on a mango leaf and soon fell fast asleep.

Early the next day, Lion began to roar, jump, and shout. He lashed his huge tail.

He pawed at his head and roared, again and again. "My ear! My ear! I am in terrible pain!"

All the animals gathered around the king.
Ant watched as each animal tried to help, but no
one could fix Lion's aching ear.

Finally, Ant bowed before Lion.

"Your majesty," she said, "perhaps I can help. Let me crawl into your ear."

Lion looked suspicious, but his pain was great. He held out his royal paw so Ant could crawl up to his ear.

Slowly the determined ant crawled through Lion's golden fur. Carefully she crawled past Lion's sharp teeth and into Lion's dark ear.

In the middle of Lion's ear, Ant stood very still and listened. Finally she heard a suspicious sound—a tiny snore.

Then Ant spied her friend, Worm. He had fallen asleep in Lion's ear!

Ant reached down and shook the sleepy Worm.

"Wake up, Worm," Ant said in her most determined voice. "I was right. Here is our chance to bow to Lion."

Ant and Worm crawled out of Lion's ear and tumbled to the ground.

The new king leaped in the air.

"The pain is gone!" he shouted. "You have saved me, little Ant. I must repay your kindness, so tell me what I can do for you. I will give you anything in my kingdom."

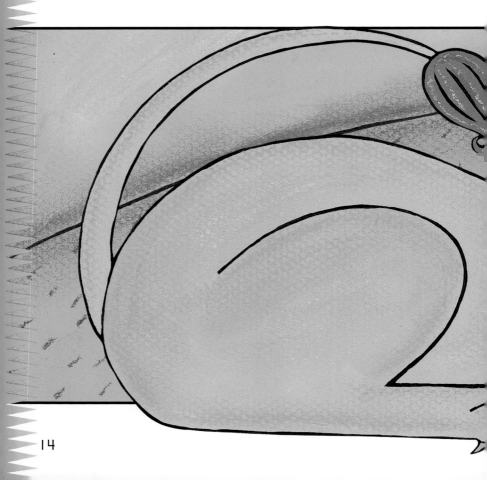

Ant bowed before Lion, and then she spoke.

"I have all that I need, Your Majesty. Now I have done the job my mother asked of me.

"But if you wish to repay me, just remember this: a small worm can cause a great deal of bitter pain, and a tiny ant can be a very valuable friend. No one is ever too small to be important."

Lion and all the animals listened to Ant's words.

Then Lion spoke. "Ant, to repay you for your service, I will give you this gift. From this day forward, all ants may go wherever they please. They may live wherever they choose, even in our homes, and no one may keep them away."

And so it is to this very day—maybe even in your own home.